The Mother &

*A Memoir:
The Warrior Queen Novelist
and Her Poet Daughter*

Liza Hyatt

Chatter House Press
Indianapolis

The Mother Poems

A Memoir:
The Warrior Queen Novelist
and Her Poet Daughter

Copyright © 2014 Liza Hyatt

Cover Design by Gary Schmitt
Schmitt Design, Inc.
schmittdesign@ymail.com

For information:

Chatter House Press
7915 S Emerson Ave, Ste B303
Indianapolis, IN 46237

chatterhousepress.com

ISBN: 978-1-937793-22-7
Library of Congress Control Number: 2014938269

For
Jane Newbold Hyatt
1934 – 2013

A mother unlike any other.

Acknowledgements

The following poems originally appeared in these publications:

Branches Magazine: Vol. 25 No. 1 (The Pear Tree)

Reckless Writing: The Modernization of Poetry by Emerging Writer's of the 21st Century, 2012
(Boats with White Sails; Mother Tongue)

Pudding Magazine: Journal of Applied Poetry #55 (Between)

The author performed three poems from this collection on May 2, 2013 at the first Indianapolis *Listen to Your Mother* show. *Listen to Your Mother* is an annual national series of original live readings celebrating motherhood. Recordings of this show are available via the following links:
http://www.youtube.com/playlist?list=PL5oPQWgVdsDkww3wTsFGa5R9oBQX-9oFX http://www.listentoyourmothershow.com/indianapolis/

Table of Contents

The Pear Tree

Following, hurrying to keep up
as she strides through pasture grass
taller than me
pausing only when she stands
shoulder to shoulder
with the old, dark tree
in the middle of the world.

She reaches into its branches,
pulls from them
something golden and shadowed,
and takes a bite.

I catch up with her,
and she hands me
this sun-warmed fruit.

Its sweet, hot, gust of juice
surprises my mouth.
Swallowing, I feel
sun, wind, wood, rain,
living food,
inside my body.

And the empty stomached
fear of being lost
is filled up by desire
to follow her,
wherever she leads,
this woman who knows the way
to this wild, sweet place,
this old, dark tree
of delicious light.

All Tied Up

The phone rings and she reaches over to answer it,
listens, says, "Ok, thanks for calling,"
talks a bit more, then hangs up.

"That was Dada," she says,
"We'll eat dinner without him.
He's all tied up at work."

I see cartoon images:
a man in a chair bound with ropes,
Bugs Bunny strapped to railroad tracks –
and expect her to hurry us out the door –
my brother, baby sister and I –
and go rescue him.

She leans back in the chair calmly.
Confused, I ask, "Are you going to untie him?"
and she laughs and explains
metaphor to me
for the first time.

And we go on with the day,
Gumby and Superfly and Mighty Mouse,
Spaghettio's for dinner,
baths with sponge goggles and bubbles,
books at bedtime,
Go Dog Go and *Are You My Mother*,
and in the morning,
Dada is there in his suit and tie,
carrying his briefcase out the door again.

And that is how things are.
He, coming and going and on his own.
She, where we live. How we live. Why we live.
He, a visitor.
She, the world.

Memory Memory

Sitting on the dryer,
banging my feet against its metal,
telling her about an image that moves in my mind,
learning from her what to call this kind of seeing,
and choosing, secretly,
to always remember
sitting on the dryer,
banging my feet against its metal,
and learning the word *memory.*

House and Home

In the crowded department store
briefly separated, I take her hand,
and look up to see the surprised face
of a strange woman saying,
"I am not your mother,"
and, embarrassed and afraid,
I look all around for the right woman,
who comes to me, laughing,
as I bury my hot face in her skirt.

Later, standing at the door to someone else's house,
waiting for her to knock,
I am shown she has a key
and learn that we are leaving home
having bought this stranger's house.

Running errands,
in the midst of moving,
I am confused and sad
when she says, "Let's go home now,"
and takes us all to the house
we have no memories of living in.

This feels as wrong to me
as calling an accidental woman "mother"
then trusting the rest of my life to her.

Where She Grew Up

One morning at Gramma and Grampa's
dairy farm in New Jersey
(which she also calls home)
she shows me how a calf
will suck on my finger,
as if I am its mother,
its thick warm tongue,
its damp breath in my palm.

Here, she says,
is where she galloped her horse through the pasture,
the Lone Ranger.

We swim in her Atlantic.
She holds me to her hip
as she strides into the wild waves
deeper than me,
stronger than me.

Almost Heard

She shows me iris, pansies,
and lily-of-the-valley
growing next to our house,
jack-in-the-pulpits in our woods.
I see darkly vibrant little people
with cloaked faces
whispering something secret
I want to hear, to understand.

One day,
amidst all these green people,
a stone throws itself from my father's lawnmower
and hits me in the knee.

That's why she notices
that both my knees are hot and swollen
long after the bruise from the stone fades.

She tells the doctor I have "knobby knees."

Later, she phones my father,
in Chicago on business,
and tells him that the doctor says
I have rheumatoid arthritis,
words I don't understand.

I move out of earshot
so I won't hear more.

Bridie Books

I am sitting under the kitchen table
with a Butterick pattern advertisement
from Harold's Department Store.
On it's pages, babies, schoolgirls,
wedding dresses, women's fashions.
The thought of becoming an adult someday
scares me,
but these women look happy,
so I begin to tell a story
about "Bridie" a little girl who goes to school,
finds a job, gets married, has a baby.

The story I am speaking aloud to myself
keeps growing as I turn the pages
and she overhears and says proudly,
"Keep that up, and someday you'll be a writer."

"What's a writer?" I ask,
and she points to the walls of books in our house
and says that, before she got married, moved to Indiana, had me,
she went to New York City
to write the Great American Novel
and that someday,
surrounded by Indiana cornfields, she still might.

From then on, though I do not yet know how to read,
I plan to write the Great American Novel for her
and the future feels less mysterious, more bearable.
All I have to do
is grow up to be a writer,
what she wants,
what she loves,
what she gave up for me.

Her Singing

She is teaching herself to play the guitar.
She plays when we are playing.
She says she can't sing
but sings anyway
filling the house
with a voice I say is beautiful.

One afternoon, she puts the guitar in the closet
and never takes it out again.

But her singing is in me,
where all the flowers have gone,
sunrise, sunset,
where all the young girls go,
blowin' in the wind,
my little one, my little one
alive, alive oh.

Skinned Knee

She and my father stand inside at the living room window
watching me attempt to ride the bike
without training wheels
down our long driveway.

I fall off, scrape my knee,
which is stiff and puffy
from the arthritis.
I sit rubbing the ache.

Years later, she will say to me,
"Your father wanted to go to you then.
But I didn't want us to coddle you
into thinking of yourself as sick, a cripple,
in a wheelchair by your senior prom.
So I told him,
'Let her tough it out.'"

Boats With White Sails

I often see her with a book
whose cover scares me with its
photo of a bull's head
sculpted from blue stone,
adorned with long gold horns.

Unable to read, one evening
I finally ask about the bull
and stories spill from her
about Crete, its palace Knossos,
the king Minos and his people the Minoans,
the princess Ariadne, the hero Theseus,
about bull-dancers, the labyrinth, the Minotaur,
a volcano, a tidal wave,
and archeologists who find the things that survive
buried underground, lost at sea.

Her words become boats with white sails
carrying me away from our living room
to Aegean islands thousands of years ago.
She shows me the book's photos of gold masks
and dolphin mosaics and figurines of
bare breasted women holding snakes
made by artists in that unreal time that really was.

I go to bed unable to sleep,
something turbulent woken in me
like a bull made of storm wave and thunder,
awe's eruption from the fault-line where
(words new to me)
history and myth overlap
and I realize that someday my own time will be lost to both
and I ache to enter the cities, the homes, the feasts and the dances
of people who lived long ago,
their stories, their hunger, their memories
fading like dreams
and still alive in our world.

Between

Pouring rain - and only swimming
will make us happy.
"Take off your clothes," she says,
"and run around naked in the yard."

I, seven, my sister five,
we hesitate.
"Go on," she urges,
like someone pushing to open a closing door.
"You're little country girls.
 Be rain nymphs!"

Leaving dresses and underwear at her feet,
we dash out into July's downpour
for the whole world to see
and every maple and hickory leaf,
every blade of grass,
even the columbines
and cosmos greet us.

Furless bodies goose bumped and shivering,
we splash and twirl,
and I lead the way to the front yard
to the lily-of-the-valley,
and the old oak I love,

just as a farmer in his truck
honks, slows to a stop,
rolls down his window,
and we hide behind the oak to see him
shake his finger at us, grinning,
and hoot something garbled and gruff
as he drives away.

Covering what we can with our arms,
we hurry to the back yard, trying
to dance as we run
but slowing until we stand
in the narrowing world,
turn our faces to the sky,
let raindrops roll down our cheeks,
and even laugh
because our sweat makes this rain
taste like tears.

Bedtime Kiss

I lean in to give her a bedtime kiss on the cheek.

She bristles, pulls away.

"Don't slobber on me," she says,
one hand holding the book I've interrupted,
the other hand wiping her cheek.

She promises to tip-toe into my bedroom
and kiss me goodnight
after I am already in bed.

I lie under the covers
resisting sleep
for as long as I am able,
listening for her.

Women's Lib

My sister and I are playing house
and she overhears us say
that because we are girls
we will grow up to become
wives and mothers.

"You don't have to get married
or have children
if you don't want to," she insists.

"You did," I say,
starting to wonder if she
wanted to.

"And I was always told
that is what girls do," she answers.
"Your generation will have more choices."

I hear regret in her voice and fight.
She is defying something,
fighting against some wound she knows
and wants to protect us from.
Understanding only that
a battle is being waged,
I ally myself with her.

Tornado

We are still emerging
with our candles from the basement
and she is already outside
looking to see the damage.

I hurry to the living room window
and watch her march purposefully,
without fear or hesitation,
up the driveway strewn
with ragged leaves and torn branches
toward the bruised sky.

One old tree I loved
has been completely uprooted
and fell just feet away
from my bedroom,
next to
instead of on
the house.

I am afraid the storm will come back for her,
or that she will walk straight to it,
choosing to leave with the tornado's turbulent strength,

unwilling to stay a second longer
pent up in her life
as my father's wife,
and our mother.

Her Blessing

She is standing on a chair
hanging a craft fair plaque
(bought while my father complained)
from a nail above the kitchen sink
which overflows with dirty dishes.

"Bless this mess,"
she says, reading the sign aloud,
laughing like a rebel
as she jumps down from the chair.

She leaves the hammer on the counter,
the dishes for later,
and we go to the basement
where her sewing table is stacked with fabric
and loose pattern pieces
and boxes of thread and rick-rack.
We listen to the radio
as the sewing machine zig-zags through corduroy
and she hums with pins between her lips
and I paint old wooden spools
turning them into disheveled Rapunzels with yarn for hair,
dripping red and yellow tempera colors
onto the already paint splattered table.

Finding Courage

I am scared to go alone into the dark, damp basement
to rescue the baby doll
left behind when she finished sewing.
But she won't go with me and tells me to
march down the basement steps singing,
"Onward Christian soldiers marching as to war!"
like she did when she was afraid.

I do and send the monsters back into the shadows
and what emboldens me the most
is not the strange and unfamiliar hymn.
It is knowing, for the first time,
that though she was fierce and tomboyish from the beginning,
she was also sometimes afraid.

Teaching

I reach out and touch dark carved wood
around a door in an old building,
a place for kings and wizards.
We are in a long line of students registering for classes.

Knowing what I am thinking, she says,
"When I first left home for Vassar,
I felt like I was going to school in a castle."
Now she is going back to school for a teaching license
and a Master's Degree in English Literature.

We visit the campus library,
the wooden heels of her Dr. Scholl sandals
striking the marble steps,
a percussive exclamation
reverberating through open floors
as she descends with a heavy stack of books.

She reads Spencer and Milton at the town swimming pool,
memorizes the prologue to the Canterbury Tales
while driving to the grocery store.
She talks at dinner about what she is learning
and I absorb the names:
Byron, Shelley, Keats,
Chaucer, Beowulf,
Shakespeare, Milton, Yeats,
Mabinogion, Tuatha de Danann,
Joseph Campbell, Bruno Bettelheim, Carl Jung.

She is teaching me that every story is the story
of the hero with a thousand faces
and that there is real magic in myth, metaphor and archetype
because the imagination is essential, healing and ancient.

When my arthritis flairs up and I am grieving,
not young and easy limbed like other kids,
I practice this teaching,
daydream I ride a white horse into a epic landscape
to fight an evil foe
and in my imagination,
I run, dance, climb, grow strong
in a body released from pain.

Trying to Change Our Bodies

She is on the living room floor doing Jack Lalanne exercises
wearing a mail-ordered pair of inflatable plastic pants
that she secretly bought, and wears now,
despite our cruel laughter,
determined to do anything
to make go away the cellulite she hates.

I try some of the exercises with her,
then, go off on my own,
where no one can see me.

Also ashamed of what I cannot control,
I try again to kneel with my legs tucked under me,
the way the other kids do so easily.
I bend my knee joints half-way
and feel burning, swollen pain,
but keep pushing down,
forcing my bottom toward my heel,
hoping that if I don't give up,
I can make the arthritis go away.

Like a Child

I am angry and disagreeable
because a drawing I am working on
doesn't look like the Michelangelo sketch
in the book I've been reading.
She asks me what is wrong with my drawing,
and I say, "It looks like a child drew it!"

"Good!" she says,
"Lots of grown-ups work
to make art as free as a child's."
I don't believe her,
so she pulls several books down from the shelves
and shows me Picasso, Matisse, Miro, and Chagall.

Later, for my birthday, she gives me
Wonders, Warriors, and Beasts Abounding,
a book about how artists see the world.
It is full of dragons and owls and frogs and whales,
sun gods and samurai,
armored knights and starry nights,
painted, sculpted, stitched and drawn
into tribal masks, medieval tapestries,
Asian scrolls, Mexican pottery, 20th century sculpture.

At the beginning of the book
is a bright yellow sun wearing black sun glasses
painted by a 5 year old boy.
We both agree it is our favorite
because it makes us laugh.

How Do You Know?

She is on the couch reading Tolkien
and I am dancing to the Carpenter's,
imagining that David Marshall,
the fastest runner in 5th grade,
watches (with growing desire)
me spin on top of the world,
looking down on creation,
the only explanation
the love we've found.

"How do you know
you love someone?" I ask her.

She looks up from the paperback and shrugs.
"You just know."

I think of the people I should love
and want to love
but for whom I have never felt anything easy or certain:
her, Dad, my brother and sister, even David.
I feel guilty and flawed –
probably for life –
because the only one I
just know I love
is Barney the Beagle.

The Summer Before 6TH Grade

This cicada evening, we sit at the dinner table
with crayons and sketch paper
drawing pictures of hobbits, dragons, elves
for the bulletin boards of her first classroom.
In fall, her 6th graders will be reading *The Hobbit*
"even if," she says,
"some of the parents with no imagination
object to stories of magic."

Other rainy summer afternoons we spend
cutting pictures from old National Geographics
and gluing them on large index cards
that her students will be given as story starters.
I want to write a story about this child holding a fish,
about this dancer leaping flames.

I will be starting 6th grade too
and, secretly, I want her
to be my teacher.

Lunar Landing

While she is in the kitchen cooking dinner,
I test my courage away from her,
venturing slowly down the dark basement steps,
my fear of monsters not quite as strong as
the lure of National Geographics
she has sorted by year
and stacked from bottom step to top,
older issues deeper down in the basement gloom –
1959 at the very bottom,
1972 at the top.

I am hunting for pictures to stir my imagination
into dreams of adventure in unknown lands,
and have come upon two covers that tell a story
beyond anything I expected.

March 1964, an artist's illustration in grey and black
of a spacesuit clad man orbiting a pale Earth:
"How We Plan to Put Man on the Moon."

December 1969, a photo, also grey and black,
of a living man standing on the real moon,
the quote, "In Peace for all Mankind"
and inside, more photos, foot-printed moon dust,
the living black of space,
the luminous blue Earth, rising.

I have a vague memory from when I was 6,
of being woken by her and made, while half asleep,
 to watch "the lunar landing" on our black and white T.V.
then going back to bed thinking this moon walk was just
another episode of Star Trek.

Now I sit in awe, seeing Earth from a perspective
that my mother could not have imagined
when she was a child,
that no one could have known until now.

There on the basement steps,
I stand with the Apollo crew
on an island of dust and rock in airless space,
looking into the blue face of our mother, our home,
for the first time conscious of the longing
that makes us ache to leave her and ache to return.

Gold Rush

When the arthritis flares up worse than before,
in all its usual places,
knees, knuckles, ankles, elbows, wrists, neck,
Dr. Gabovitch recommends gold salt treatments.

At first once a week,
then every two, every three, once a month,
for all of sixth and much of seventh grade,
she drives me after school
to the clinic near the old city hospital
where my blood is drawn,
and I pee into a urine sample cup,
and then bare my bottom
for the same, short crabby nurse
who stabs me with a needle
injecting muscle with what I bravely imagine
is living, magic gold.

The drive is 40 minutes, each way,
from our white suburbs
(where people are moving to avoid desegregation)
past increasingly run-down houses and apartments.

In the clinic waiting room, I am always the only child.
I sit looking at tired faces,
people with canes and special shoes,
wondering what is wrong with them,
wondering if I will be like them when I am older.

But the swelling is fading, first from my neck, then elbows, then wrists,
the arthritis draining from my body
like sand from an hourglass,
and on the drive home, despite my sore butt cheek,
I feel a kind of warm, golden glow,
that sudden elation other kids seem to feel often
and take for granted,

and even though there is homework,
the rush-hour drive, papers to grade, dinner to fix,
she will often stop at a burger place,
and buy me a root beer to-go
which I'll sip slowly
trying to make this amber fizz last
the entire drive home.

Sidelines

She is teaching us to play tennis.
She returns my weak lob
with a strong back-hand
which I scramble to reach,
feeling my racquet sift through empty air.

I protest that I need an easier volley and she says,
"By your age, I knew how to compete."

This summer both my brother and my sister play Little League,
the first year girls have teams.
I watch from the sidelines,
the girl with the knobby knees
for whom sports are painful and embarrassing.

She signs me up for art lessons.
The first three letters of arthritis are A-R-T.

Puberty

Whenever she talks about her childhood,
she remembers the horse her father gave her
and how she galloped
through the farm pastures every day,
sharing with Pilot alone her secrets and sorrows,
even finding, I have recently learned,
her first menstrual flow
after a July day in his saddle.

So, when our neighbor decides to sell his horse,
she buys Brandybuck for us,
and I spend the summer
learning to groom and feed and gallop him,
and am oddly pleased -
because it is a kind of sharing with her –
to find, after coming in from a sweaty ride,
the first streak of blood
in my underwear.

Physical Contact I Remember Outgrowing

Bouncing me on her knee for
"this is the way the ladies ride, trit-trot, trit- trot."
Holding my hand to walk across the street.
Pushing me in a swing.
Feeling my forehead for a temperature.
Holding me with both hands under my back while I learned to float.
Helping me learn to ride the waves.
Paddling me for not cleaning my room.
Giving me butterfly kisses.
Washing my hair,
cutting my hair into pixie cuts, and uneven bangs.
Fighting out the tangles in my hair after I grew it long.

Today, my Laura Ingalls Wilder braid
will be cut into a Dorothy Hamill wedge
at the beauty salon.

I do not know it yet
but it is already normal
for us not to touch.

The Fight

We've eaten dinner on the screen porch
and have gone inside to watch t.v.
leaving her and my father talking outside
as dusk settles into night.

Suddenly I hear sounds of shouting
and then glass breaking
over the sirens of my favorite show,
Emergency.

I go to the porch door and open it.
My mother is standing,
as if she had been starting to run,
and oily dressing and lettuce,
are flung across the cement floor,
the glass salad bowl,
broken in many pieces,
at her feet.

She sees me and knows I see her alarm
and says, "It's alright.
We are just having a disagreement.
Go back inside."

I do what she says,
reluctantly closing the door.

Because my father asked her to,
my mother has served
salad for our dinner
every night of our entire lives,
chopping vegetables in the kitchen
while he sipped his whisky and read in the living room,
bringing him the root base of the heart of the celery
to suck on as he likes to do.

Her homemade oil-and-vinegar dressing
is sour and puckery and I can smell it
in the air now
the way I could smell in the house for weeks
the sap of the tree beside my bedroom window
ripped down and torn open by the tornado.

And for the first time in my life
I wonder why my father never helps make the salad,
why they never kiss or laugh
or tease each other in front of us
and I wonder what they are arguing about,
and wish I could see more of their fight,
frightened, but glad,
to have had this one glimpse
of passion between them.

Mother Tongue

On our pilgrimages to the grocery store
when I was still learning to read,
she taught me Chaucer -
Whan that Aprill with his shoures soote…
We bought Ding Dongs and Tab and Life Cereal
then drove home repeating
the droghte of March hath perced to the roote
and she explained how languages change over time
and bathed every veyne in swich licour.

During a summer cook-out, she convinced
my brother's Little League team that she was a witch:
Boil, boil, toil, and trouble,
fire burn and cauldron bubble.

Now, when other mothers are introducing their teens
to manicures, waxes, and color treatments at the salon,
she enrolls us together
in a Free University Anglo-Saxon class –
weord weorold –
the only students on the worn couch
of an effeminate linguist
who lives with his identical twin.

At dinner, she teaches us the Norman invasion of 1066
is why civilized folk eat poultry, pork and beef –
le poulet, le porc, et le boeuf –
not the chickens, hogs, or cows
that shit and fuck in the stables.

She likes to swear *"God damn it all to hell!"* when really pissed off
and admits she has little use for the mediocrity of the masses.
Failing students, slow drivers, people with poor grammar,
slow crowds leaving baseball games or summer fireworks with coolers and lawn-chairs
are *yahoos, troglodytes, baboons, imbeciles.*

There are still times I lie awake
listening for the sound of her voice in a far room,
the cadence of half-heard words,
all language unlearned as I fall asleep,
changing back into rhythm, poetry,
a wombed song without need of meaning.

What I Know

I know that she doesn't like her thighs, dimpled with cellulite.

I know that when she was my age
she played lacrosse at school,
and was teased by her siblings about "Mighty Dwighty"
the boy she had raft fights with at the beach club,
their mutual attraction made known
when he threw a dead rabbit at her to see if she'd squeal
and she'd picked it up and hurled it right back at him.

I know that, even then, she felt big, red-haired, smart
and not at all pretty or girlish.

I know that I feel invisible, alone, unathletic,
and that I am afraid even to speak to boys,
let alone throw anything at them, living or dead.

I know that from time to time she will point to a woman in a store
and ask, "Am I that fat?"

I know that I want my breasts to look like hers
but I do not want her butt.

I know that she has freckles on the back of her shoulders.

I know that she has a copy of *The Joy of Sex* under her bed.

I know that she is falling for a friend of my father's,
a musician 15 years younger than her.

I know that this same man, 15 years older than me,
is behind me in the hallway where no one can see us,
is kissing me on the back of my neck and whispering,
"Don't be afraid. I love you."

I know that I am drawn to him like no girlish crush,
that I don't know what love is,
but would give him my body, my hidden heart
to play upon for better or worse.

I know that I am pulling away, rushing to a place of safety,
that she wants him to love her,
that I must not compete.

Wild Berries

The arthritis has not flared up again for three years.
I begin to let myself believe
that the disease is really gone.
I begin to relax,
to wonder what pleasure
my body can feel instead of pain,
to trust it is my time to explore.

Wild black raspberries grow
in the woods encircling our house.
On dew-wet mornings, I pick them
secretly thinking of the uneven texture
of a woman's ruddy nipples,
of my own new-grown breasts,
of being touched there by a man.

I pick the berries knowing he will eat them,
the musician we both love.
I bring them in, wet and ripe
and she bakes them into a pie,
and he, our guest for dinner,
swallows their warm, red pulp and juice,
and composes songs on our piano
as full of secrets and longing
as my changing body.

Sweet Sixteen

My birthday comes at the beginning of December.
Instead of a sweet-16 gold and diamond necklace
like my friends' parents have given them,
she gives me antique brass bookends shaped like unicorns.

A few weeks later, her father dies in his sleep on Christmas night.
She returns from the funeral and asks for a divorce
saying that on the plane flight home
she kept thinking, *Who needs this shit?*
She buys a house in the city,
a few blocks from our musician friend,
and near the end of winter she moves there.

Our home, the black raspberries, the horse, the trees,
the spring-beauties and the place near the woods
where Barney the Beagle is buried,
is sold.
The world I have known is lost,
everything divided,
childhood toys, the basement's National Geographics,
given to Goodwill.

I want to stay home.
I have no choice but to leave it and go with her.

Her Hands

She is on her feet all day in the classroom.
At home, she throws the navy pumps or penny loafers
she lectured in all day
into the mound of shoes piled on her closet floor
and sits with words in her lap,
grading essays, writing, reading.

I watch her hands.
She is always touching something,
holding a pen,
turning a page,
picking at dry skin around her thumbnail.

Her hands know how to:
guide fabric past the rapid sewing machine needle,
pound the dinner table to emphasize a point,
saddle a horse,
embroider,
wring the neck of a chicken,
apply lipstick,
pinch a gorged tick from behind the ear of the dog,
bridge shuffle a deck of cards,
knit,
shift gears in the car,
light and smoke a cigarette (a college habit,
given up for my father, rebelliously reclaimed),
tap off ashes, extinguish the butt,
clean up cat puke,
press a blouse,
ignore grease spatters and singed skin while cooking,
lay out and pin a pattern to fabric,
gather a ruffle on a skirt,
taunt the cat to claw her,
gesture as she speaks, turning words into invisible swords.

Often she lays the long arc made by index finger and thumb
under her right breast,
her ragged-edged thumb resting on her sternum
holding herself in a way that looks unconsciously comforting.

Her Father's Daughter

Her mother out-lives her father by a few years.
She goes to visit her alone,
insisting that if we were there
Gramma would only point out
our flaws and her faults as a mother.
When she comes home from these visits, she says,
"When I am her age,
remind me that I intend to do more
than complain and criticize!"

As I watch her grieve her father
and endure her mother,
I learn little details about her life.
Her father read to her as a child,
making special voices for each character,
demanding she think, explore, learn.
Her mother sighed with displeasure,
drank daily, and warned my mother
that thinking too deeply could drive a person crazy.
Her father liked to argue, bellow,
and pierce with sarcastic barbs,
and it was he she lived to please
because it was he who loved her mind.

Walls and Equations

She has taken a second job
teaching "bone-head" English
to college freshmen in night school.

My sister and I are alone
in the house of thick brick walls
she moved us to with her divorce.

I am alone in this house after feeling alone at school all day,
surrounded by teen cliques, more impenetrable than brick walls,
while my best friend spends all her time with a new boyfriend.

I am in my bedroom by myself
doing calculus and physics homework,
solving math equations for acceleration,
all the while trying to understand the love equation.

Finally she is home one night and I make her listen to
the relationship math I have worked out.
To find love, I say,
I need to have been given love
so that I have some of it to share.
But all she seems to want for herself and for me
is independence.
So won't I always be alone?

She is tired and angry and says I am being overly dramatic.
She says I will know love someday.
She doesn't understand I need it now.
I have to ask her if she loves me.
She says, "Of course I do" with irritation.

Active Imagination

During her divorce, she writes a story
about a childless queen who loves a minstrel
who is killed by the jealous king.
And then the queen discovers
the king in the arms of a young wench.
And so she turns to old magic,
becomes an eagle, strong and fierce,
soars and screams within turbulent storms over mountain and sea,
and destroys the kingdom's sheep in nightly rampages of grief and rage
until, at last, the king's own arrow kills her.
It is the story of an aging woman in a loveless marriage
who unleashes pent-up, wild fury,
willing to destroy everything, even her old life,
in order to be free.

After her divorce, my grieving body is again
the unwilling host to something dark and painful.
Hating the brick city house surrounded by brick city houses
where she has moved us,
when I close my eyes,
I see a starving girl, hauntingly hungry.
For weeks, whenever this image surfaces, I push it away.
Finally, I ask the girl what she needs.
She shows me she is surrounded by
a circular stone wall that is too tall to climb
and has no door.
The garden within, which used to nourish her, is dying.
The girl kneels on the ground next to the wall, her strength failing.
"Dig," I tell her, and she begins to claw at the ground,
making a tunnel under the rocks,
bringing us both back to life.

In The Mall

I hurry to match her stride,
but she, always two feet in front of me,
walks with long, impatient steps,
passing everyone.

At this age,
I should be pulling away from her.

But she has always kept a distance

and I am still trying to close the gap.

Conquests

Since her divorce, she talks about *conquests.*
The musician she left her marriage for,
the Thoreau scholar who lives with his mother,
the crazy professor in Iowa from the Singles Booklovers Club.
They have loud sex when he first visits.

One Saturday, two minutes after
the crazy professor hits the road,
the Thoreau scholar arrives unexpectedly.

As we watch him come toward the door,
she says proudly,
"One Tom cat leaves and another saunters up on the prowl.
I should buy a pistol
so I can start marking notches in it."

Her Advice

Home after the first semester of college
in far-from-her Sante Fe,
Land of Enchantment, Sangre de Cristos,
I stand in her kitchen
telling her that I am going to have sex
with the young man at school
who I know I love.

I want something from her wise and nurturing,
a rite of passage gift.

She says, "Use protection," with practical brevity.

And then, "Sex is something that once you start, you have to have."

Needing more, I ask what she means.

She says, "For me, there is just nothing as powerful,"
bragging, still far ahead
in a competition
I never even entered.

Gypsy

When she comes to visit,
we talk about Don Quixote, Dante, D.H. Lawrence.

She asks little about my boyfriends or breakups,
refusing, she says, to be "like the other mothers
hurrying their daughters into marriage
so they can have grandkids."

We go shopping and she buys me
tiered skirts, fringed and beaded scarves,
flowing rayon,
Indian cotton dresses with sequins and bells,
Tarot cards,
the journals of Anais Nin,
Indian moccasins.

Whenever she visits, I live in a different place,
with different roommates.
I say I like being a gypsy,
because home,
even in my own body,
feels impossible,
and playing free-spirit
keeps me from knowing
how full my body is
with discontent
and longing.

Need

After graduating,
I move in with another boyfriend,
this one younger than me, still in school.

She visits
and while I am at work,
a health food store cashier,
she reads the books on women's psychology
piled on my desk.

She tells me that until now
she hasn't known what it means to be a woman.
That I am far wiser than her at my age.

My boyfriend comes home from studying with friends.
When he undresses, I mistake his scent as desire for me.
While my mother sleeps in the other room,
I suck his cock hard,
surprised by the taste of semen and another's cunt.
I say nothing, open my legs to him,
not knowing what, or whose, need I am trying to feed.

After the Land of Enchantment

After leaving the Land of Enchantment,
I sit on the rim of the Grand Canyon
and feel more hollow than it,
try living in Oregon, in the corner of the world,
further west than Independence.
She has offered to pay my way to Zurich to study Jung
but I just can't keep gypsying.

Not sure if I am moving back –
or if I'll be leaving as soon as I know a better place to go –
I ship boxes of books
and drive my car-full of belongings
to her house.

I am fasting,
trying to shrink my hips and thighs,
trying to not become her,
trying to slow time down,
to feel young again,
to feel vibrant again.

I tell her about standing alone
on the Pacific shore, Christmas day.
About the waves, the wind, gull flight, sand striations,
arcs of foam and shell,
and their recurrent motion and shape
in which it seemed that ultimate meaning,
a total wholeness of all,
is written, is spoken by Earth,
and was, on that shore,
almost understood by something arcing deeper in me
than grief and longing.
I tell her that as I stood there,
on the verge of understanding everything,
I felt a sudden eruption of loving
rushing toward me from the edge of space,
rushing out from the deep center.
Not God, I say. Godding.

I tell her I need to hold on to that.
I need to live my life for that.

She sighs. "You can't be a guru.
Do something practical.
Find god while folding the laundry."

Leaving

She is carrying a box downstairs,
catches her heal, twists,
and she and the box go falling.

I am still in town, in grad school,
and she is leaving her house in my hands
to go live two states away
with her Single-Booklovers-Club lover
who dumped her for one of his students
but has now returned years later, repentant.

I approach, ask if I can help.
She sits, rubbing her ankle impatiently.

It is as if I am the mother
and she is the young woman
rebelling by eloping with a man
I don't approve of.

"I'm fine, I'm fine," she insists.
"Just get out of my way.
I've got to get the hell out of here!"

She stands and picks up the box,
kicks away the books that have spilled from it,
pushes down the steps
refusing to notice any evidence of injury.

Switched Places

Living in her house,
too full of something old and furious,
I diet compulsively
trying not to feel,
trying not to turn into her,
until my period fails to come.
I date but feel no passion,
reject one proposal,
have empty angry sex with a married man.
Hollow, hungry, desireless,
not even 30, I feel like a menopausal woman,
grieving because the whole world reminds me
of lost, and unlived, youth.

She sends me news of life in Iowa with the crazy professor.
Living on the land. Coyotes and prairie moons.
Beer and long debates by the campfire.
Sex under the stars.
In one photo, she is drenched with summer sweat,
tan, braless, her white tee-shirt clinging to her breasts,
the free-spirit hippie
she was too married and child-bound
in the 70's to be.
In another photo
she's in a claw-footed bathtub on the back of his pick-up,
her bare arm raised in triumph,
a fierce look on her face,
the Viking queen in her boat.

Bless This Mess

For the life they've planned,
she sells her house.
I rent an apartment, she rents a storage unit,
and hurries back to Iowa.

Two months later, the love of her life
is a lying alcoholic,
his "research trip to Mexico" spent in Florida
with someone named Sherry.

I make myself eat, go to therapy.
She joins Al-Anon,
we read about codependency,
admit to being armored and hard to get close to.

I ask if she will return to live near me.
She says if she were close
she would poison my relationships.

She moves to New Mexico.
Sangre de Cristo.
Blood of Christ,
blood of the virgin, of first love,
blood of gypsy youth,
blood of grief,
blood of shadow,
mother shadow, witches' curse, never escape,
she is in my blood,
mess, mess, bless, bless,
every twist and tangle of vein, every cell of our blood.

Storm, Tree – Fire, Air – Earth, Moon

She is a storm.
I am a tree, bending, bending.

She is fire.
I am oxygen.

She is the fire-breathing dragon,
guarding the heap of her life.
I am the treasure she needs and crushes.

She is a Viking queen.
I am her shame,
the child whose birth
lessened her into the life of woman.

She is the Earth.
Caught in her wake,
I am the moon.

Pulled into her, repelled by her.
Attracted, yearning to break free.

This separation, this perfect distance –
need it, make it so.

I have to amass my own self, feel my own weight,
chart a course on her periphery.

Better to slip in and out of her shadow
than to be a meteor
sucked in and ground to dust.

The Announcement

We sit at the kitchen table
in the house I share with a man
I plan to marry, to muddle through with,
learning to love, by trial and error.

I tell her,
"I've decided to get married.
It is time I stay with someone."

She looks over her glasses and responds,
"Why?"

The Wedding

It is a beautiful May afternoon.

The music is played by an old friend -
the man she and I both loved
when she was 44, he 30, me 15.

The reception is a blur of people.

The tree we asked everyone to hug
is covered with poison ivy.

Before we say our vows,
she reads the passage from Rilke I've chosen.
She speaks carefully, firmly, projecting so all hear:

And so loving, for a long while ahead,
and far on into life is –
solitude,
intensified and deepened loneness
for she who loves.

At a Crossroads

Time is running out if I am going to have a baby.

I've lived afraid of:
more pain,
losing control,
getting fat,
looking like her,
being like her,
giving up like her before becoming the writer we both wanted to be,
failing,
being less than.

I've lived afraid of her disapproval,
of not achieving the *more* she wanted,
when she told my sister and I
that women could be so much more
than mothers.

But there was another moment, in childhood,
when I had a vision of myself a woman,
crossing a city street, hand in hand
with a little girl, who was mine,
the two of us walking away from the field of sight,
into the future, the unknown.

I keep returning secretly to that vision.

The desire for that crossroads, that girl
is stronger than any of those old fears.

Becoming the Mother

At the first sound of the heartbeat through the doptone,
I laugh, utterly baffled by this joy
as it came suddenly, uncontrollably,
from a place inside myself I do not know,
the way I used to laugh when I orgasmed,
only from even deeper in my core.

I see my mother once as my belly rounds,
in the 7th month, at my brother's wedding.
Back home, a friend my mother's age,
says I seem deeply contented.
I ask her to be my adopted mother.

I savor the pregnancy, the secret intimacy
that I alone share with my unborn child.

After 30 some hours in labor and still not fully dilated,
I need to know what is holding me back.
The inner answer: My fear.
What if I am just like *her?*

And finally I see this hesitation in everything I do,
every day, every moment, hindered by this fear,
unfair, a chokehold.
I am not her! I pray. *This is my child
and I will be the mother I will be!*

And all I want now is life.
My child's.
My own.

At First Sight

More than once, as a child I asked:
What was it like when I was born?
And she answered:
You were blue and made a face like this...
(Demonstrating, like repeatedly trying to spit out something rancid.)

I am already telling my daughter this:
I cannot take my eyes off you, my Maggie,
from the first glimpse of you, like a seal
leaving your first sea for me your shore
and now, in your first seconds, hours, days, weeks,
every time I look at you
all I see is love.

Her First Visit

When she visits, she tells me this story
about her own mother's first visit
to see her newborn grandchild:
"When we arrived home from the airport,
I said 'lunch needs to be fixed and the baby needs a bottle'
and my mother said, 'I'll get the lunch.
I've never handled a bottle in my life.
There were servants to tend to that.'"

I wonder how often my mother's mother held her.

She doesn't hold Maggie even once.

I am not surprised and –
aside from an old longing
for a more mothered kind of mother –
am not bothered.

I don't want anyone but me to hold my baby.

The Gifts She Gives Us

She shows her fondness by giving us books and art.

She buys us the complete A.A. Milne
so I can read aloud "James James Morrison Morrison"
like she did for me.

She finds her own favorite childhood story –
Elsie Piddock Skips in Her Sleep –
is back in print, and ships us a copy.
It is about a girl taught to jump rope by the fairies
and whenever I read it, I get tearful,
the way she always does when she hears bag-pipes.

She won't go with us, because her hip is bothering her,
but, while visiting, watches from the window
as I and my toddler girl
take the dog on a winter's walk.

Months later, a picture she has drawn from memory
arrives in the mail –
of me and my little girl, barely taller than my knee,
walking hand-in-hand
as we cross a street,
walking toward the future, the unknown.

With the picture, she sends a note:
Always made me cry thinking of kind little Hobbits
going out to battle Mordor.
Still think of you that way
and wish I could smooth the way.
You know where you are going
and will take Maggie along.
Let me know if I can help."

How She Was Right, Years Ago

My husband has never pulled a book from my shelves in curiosity
and attempts to talk about "soul" and "spirituality,"
even after I've learned to not use those words,
inflame his skepticism and cause arguments.
He wants me to appreciate that he changes the oil in my car
and pulls weeds from the driveway.
He wants fewer wrinkles in his permanent press.

And so, I seek the transcendent
in my love for my daughter,
in work, and in friendships away from home.
When I return,
instead of hoping, trying, failing
to share with him any of the stirred embers of my old awe,
I find solace in the basement
where I ground myself, clean the litter box,
gather the darks from the dryer
and start to fold,
accepting that my mother was right all those years ago:
After enlightenment, the laundry.

The Years Pass

And my husband and I repeat the same argument,
my mother and I the same distant orbits.

She visits once or twice a year
and she insists I not change
my work or routines with Maggie,
that she is perfectly content
doing crosswords at the kitchen table.

She complains that her hip is bothering her
because the plane was too cramped,
the futon too hard,
the mattress too soft,
or her new orthodics made incorrectly.

She sits on a bench outside the library,
in the museum, at the park, in the car,
wherever possible, smoking.

When Maggie is asleep and my husband out,
she criticizes my husband
for being too angry and critical,
complains about how worthless most men are
and says that it is a good thing she lives so far away
so I can muddle through on my own without her negativity
because she wouldn't put up with it
and I am much more patient than she ever was.

When she leaves,
I feel hardened and exhausted,
glad for how easily and surely I love Maggie,
and resolved to keep working
in therapy and couple's counseling
for whatever kind of imperfect intimacy
remains possible for me in marriage.

What We Write

She self-publishes one memoir, six novels,
a collection of short stories.
She sends me autographed copies and insists
that the unhappy daughters (and their clueless husbands)
are not exactly
based on me, or mine,
but the descriptions are too accurate, and too inaccurate,
and therefore too painful,
so I read in full only the novels that take place
in the English Middle Ages.

I struggle and always feel that I am failing
to hold onto poetry.
When the baby is small,
I write poems about what I see
in one square foot of land next to the house,
the gas-meter, the winter bloomed pansy,
Persephone's pomegranate from the compost pile.
As the baby grows
and I surrender my creativity to mothering
and my failing marriage demands what energy I have left,
I write angry, preachy poems about life in the suburbs,
road-kill and loss of nature.
I write about dreams
of hollow men and dead leaves,
of crossroads and red shoes,
of executions and tear-filled grails,
of deer who want me to follow them to an uncivilized time,
of a starving woman who turns into a mountain lion.
I write two poems in which a lover I wish I had speaks to me:
I will massage the places in you that have turned to concrete
so that you can become again
soft as mud.

She reads whatever I send her.

Warmth Against Stone

After ten years of marriage,
almost divorcing twice,
five years of couples' counseling,
I've learned this much:

I married believing I was too much like my mother
to be good at loving.

Like a waif trying to warm herself against a cold stone wall,
I married someone emotionally armored like my mother,
anxious and afraid of change or conflict like my father.

And it goes both ways –
I keep hurting him too,
the way his parents hurt him.

I thought my only hope was to endure
my heart's arthritic stance,
to bend it, force it, despite the pain,
to work at love since love is work.

With my daughter I have discovered
I am capable of softness, tenderness, quiet nurturing,
and my love is easy, generous, glad.

And so when someone who knew me and my mother
when I was a child,
when the musician who played at my wedding,
when our 'old family friend' (now my daughter's piano teacher)
puts one of my poems to music and
tells me he has always loved me
that I deserve to know love
that he will leave his marriage to be with me when I leave mine
I believe after all these years of being lost,
I am finally coming home.

My mother is the first I tell.
When she hears what I have chosen,
she offers no words of warning or caution.
She says, "Good. However this unfolds, you won't regret it."

Love Song Revised

Within three months of walking out of our marriages
into a house we promise to share for the rest of our lives,
the man I've been calling 'the love of my life'
tells me he is leaving
and I discover that my mother and I were, of course,
not the only unhappily married women
from whom he sought consolation
and that one of them is now his refuge from me.

And then he is gone, accusing me of over-reacting,
leaving his piano, his books, his still-packed boxes,
the folk harp he built for me behind.

My mother arrives for her yearly visit.
While we are out looking for houses I can afford alone,
he comes and trucks away everything
but the piano, which will require movers,
and the harp, the only thing he's given me that I will keep.

On the piano, I find an open folder of songs he has composed,
a few with my poems,
and, amongst the yellowed pages,
one with lyrics written in my mother's hand in 1980
about how he freed her from her own unhappiness,
how she will always love him, though there are other women.

Beside my mother's lines, I write my own verses
and slip them in the folder for him to find:
Love is precious because it's mortal.
Mine for you has lived so long. So long.
This love, at long last nears death's portal
Do not resuscitate. End this song.

The Scar

After I settle into my new place,
she visits again
to see how I am doing.

"I'm so proud of how strong you are,"
she says with an imposing scowl
from the head of my kitchen table,
to me, at her right, where I sat as a child.
"You're handling things just fine
and don't need a bit of help."
She pushes away her breakfast dishes
and begins the crossword puzzle.

She's lived unmarried for 30 years,
and this stern approval,
is the only comfort she will give
so I do not tell her
how afraid and torn open I am,
but let her talk again
about why I will like living alone
as I study the scar on the back of her hand.

I was eight. In her kitchen.
A sudden splash of frying pan grease
melting her skin from knuckles to wrist.
In her eyes, tears almost sizzled
as she willed them away,
angry that I saw them,
as she pushed past me,
rubbed butter on the burn,
and kept working.

For days after,
I sat beside her at family meals,
silently observing the never-mentioned burned place
turn pink, raw, weepy,
wanting a soft, open place in her,
failing to reach out, to heal her,
to understand the scarred edges of her love,
colluding with her inconsolable need for strength.

Writer's Block

I can't write.
Don't want to write.
Don't want to be a writer.

I don't want to lug these heavy boxes
of notebooks, folders, files, and unfinished rough drafts
around with me any more,
some written when I was 13, 6, 10 (my daughter's age now).
I envy the girl I was, her eager imagination,
her love of words, her creativity,
see and love these in my daughter,
fear that what is left for me
is a bitter silence, distrust, disgust.

I put piles and piles of old writing
in the recycling bin on the curb
and no one notices or cares when it is gone.

I begin learning to play the harp,
savoring its wordless resonance
as I hold it to my chest,
playing for Maggie as she falls asleep.

Friends tell me to write about the divorce,
the fantasy love, the heart break,
Writing, they say, as I've told them before,
will be healing.

And so I write:
"When we were in our early 40's,
my mother and I each
became the lover of the same man,
leaving our marriages for him."

And then I stop.

I start again:
"Keep that up and someday you'll be a writer,"
my mother said to me before I could even read.
"What's a writer?" I asked...

Whose story have I been living, hers or mine?

Unexpected Forgiveness

I sit on a cushion in my bedroom, meditating.
Quiet, wordless being.

My mother comes to mind.

How hard she is to love.

And suddenly I see –

I have always loved her,
have made every choice trying to earn her love.

And have received it.

For what she *can* love,
for what had been loved in her,
her father's gifts:
intelligence, wit, skill with words,
independence, stubborn strength.

I start to cry,
forgiving her at last
for how she was not loved,
for how she was not mothered,
for how she could not mother.

Lone Ranger

As is our routine,
she tells me when her plane arrives
and to look for her outside smoking
near the baggage claim,
no need to meet her at the gate
with all the other hugging families.

But at the airport, the only person sitting outside,
looking away from the people coming and going,
is an old cowboy with a long wheat-white pony tale,
a cane, a baggy man's coat, and scuffed, muddy shoes.

I hurry inside, go to the Southwest ticket desk
to see if she boarded the plane,
have her paged, look outside again,
and find the old cowboy, starting another cigarette,
is angry,
is her.

I wheel her luggage to my car as she hobbles behind me.
After all her impatience with people walking too slowly,
she is now impatient with me
for walking too fast.

At my house, she hobbles from bedroom to table to coffee pot
without her cane
by gripping the backs of chairs, the kitchen counter.

For her return flight, she insists
on being left at the curb.
As we say goodbye, I surprise us both
by saying "I love you," and giving her a big hug,
which she returns, unprepared, off-balance.

We pull away quickly
and I realize forgiveness
includes accepting
what cannot change.

This is the way we are with each other.
After so many years,
sharing this trail as we have, kemo sabe,
the joints of our relationship are stiff,
inflexible, set.

Assisted Living Tour

My sister and I arrange a tour
of the retirement village a few miles down the road from my house.
My sister drives from Massachusetts with her husband.
This will be the first time the three of us, mother and daughters,
have spent a week together since my sister left for college.

I get Mom at the airport, outside the gate this time,
where I watch a sky-cap bringing her down the corridor
in an airport wheelchair.
The words 'dowager queen' come to mind
to describe how she is holding court with this young man, her servant.
I take over, wheeling my mother into the elevator, feeling panic,
doing what has never been allowed before,
helping her.

We leave the chair at the baggage claim
and to get to my car, she uses her cane
and holds my arm for support
and in her grip, I feel her anger for needing me
and for my panic at being touched by her in need.

During the week-long visit, my sister and I
let her husband be the gentleman
by offering our mother his arm,
and more than once she says so we can hear,
"What a fine son-in-law you are,
unlike my daughters
who won't help their aged mother."

At the retirement village, she asks me point blank,
in front of our guide –
to whom she has made it perfectly clear
that she in no way
considers herself in need of such a place –
"And if I move here, how often will you come to visit?"
Caught off guard, I respond, "More often than I do now."

Back home, she says the retirement village
is too full of old white people for her taste
and that she is determined to live on her own until 2012
because that is the Mayan date
for the end of the world.

My sister and I do the hard thing,
enter the argument she wants to have,
tell her if she insists on living alone
then she needs to go to a different doctor,
get new advice about a hip replacement,
stop smoking, go for walks,
get someone to come around regularly to help her.
"I don't need help. I don't want to go for a walk," she snaps.
"I don't need a hip replacement," she yells.

My sister keeps bringing up how uninvolved in our lives she is,
and finally Mom says that it is *my* fault she moved far away from us
because I told her once
that she took all the oxygen from the room.

I sit next to her thinking,
This is what happens when a fire-breathing dragon gets old.

I watch us playing today's versions of the parts we have always had.
She pushes away, rips eagle claws
through any hint of vulnerability,
suffers indignantly while making it too dangerous to help.
My sister demands she change.
I detach, give in to what she wants,
independence at all cost,
realizing that now means giving her
the freedom to set her apartment ablaze smoking in bed,
to be found decaying amid heaps of books by a woman from her bridge club
who wonders why they haven't heard from her for a few weeks.
They will phone me, the daughter guilty of letting her mother die that way,
the daughter that took care of her mother
by not taking care of her mother.

Fallout

After that visit, my sister and I don't call her for several weeks.
She does not call either.
Finally a letter arrives from her full of anger.
For not helping her.
For telling her she wasn't managing well enough on her own.

I write back saying, "I do not know how
to help you and leave you alone at the same time.
If there are specific things I can do to help, please tell me."

Exactly a year after the big argument
she calls my sister and I to say,
"I am at my friend Kate's house,
recuperating from hip replacement surgery."

We find out she has known for months the date of the surgery
and she said nothing about it.
"You don't need to come attend to me.
Kate is controlling everything to an extreme as it is."

As the weeks pass, she tell us that
her landlord Ivan is helping her clean her apartment,
so she can't find anything now.
She has been placed on oxygen
and hasn't smoked since the surgery.
She is walking a bit every day,
but not as far as she should,
according to her friend Kate,
who misunderstands all the doctor's instructions.
But that doesn't matter
because Kate has stopped speaking to her,
though she doesn't know why.

I Write Because

I start to write about how my mother moved through this world.

I write about trying to catch up with her
as she (my age now) tore impatiently past
all the stupid people in the mall.

I write about her last visit and how,
the day before the argument,
we went to 4th of July fireworks
and she was unable to walk, even with her cane,
the parking lot distance
between my car and the sidewalk,
how she sat on the cooler,
fuming, as people pushed past us.

I write about how she moved
because my life first moved
within her body, from her body
and has always moved with her, from her,
trying to leave her, but always following.

I write because I want to understand how we got here.

I write poems I don't want to ever let her see,
and still somehow, I am
communicating with her through them.

I write because I don't enjoy our phone calls
which she uses to criticize the people around her
(the hip surgery hospital staff, the physical therapist,
the people at Walmart).

I write because I've always written to connect to her.

I write because I want to understand what she feels
having entered the last decade of her life.

I write because I am the same age she was
when she chose her own difficult self,
even though that choice conflicted irreparably
with being wife, and mother.

I write because my daughter is growing
more and more independent
and I feel her pushing me away,
and I want her to separate–
I want my own independence back –
and I want her to need me –
and I hate how our bond has become complicated,
never again easy,
and I write to remember
how this transition forced its way
into my life before
when I was the child.

I write because I need to see
what was beautiful, what was blundering,
what was giving, what was painful,
what was difficult, and what came easily
in this dance we've been doing
for almost 5 decades.

I write because I feel
that dance winding down,
no more jitterbug or rock-and-roll,
a slowing waltz
nearing its final measures.

Family Time

My sister hosts us all for a week
after her son's high school graduation.
Mom, Dad, my brother, and I,
all in the same house,
all sleeping under the same roof
for the first time since before my parent's divorce
three decades ago.

My sister's kitchen table,
the hub of the wheel
where all of us,
all of us,
come together
trying to get along
despite the tension between and within us.

Other families do this regularly
for birthdays, for Thanksgiving,
year after year,
while our family last gathered,
all of us at the kitchen table,
when I was sixteen years old.

In the middle of a day in the middle of this visit,
my mother asks if my sister or I would
trim her toenails.

I hesitate,
startled to be asked this task,
after all these years
of avoiding each other,
wondering if I can
work up the courage
to kneel down in my sister's kitchen

with the rest of the family all gathered around
and touch my mother's arthritic feet,
and tend her old jagged, yellow claws,
so opposite from a baby's,
the only human nails
besides my own
that I have trimmed.

Before we can answer,
she snaps, "Never mind!
I should have known
you'd be afraid to help."

I say nothing, regretful
about all of this,
everything we will never do for each other,
and very much relieved
that she will now
petulantly refuse
any help
I might have offered.

The Song

On the floor, weeping again,
up from the belly,
each breath sounding the depth.
Old ground gone.
Old sound.
Deeper.

My mother – almost eighty, health fading.
My daughter – fifteen, strong wings, rarely home.

The two females I've loved
with my body –
life depending on it –
are leaving me.

When my wild heart calms
I go to the woods.
To the ridge over the creek,
the new hepatica – ephemeral flowers –
love them now before they are gone –
and robins, dusk, spring frogs,
their slow rattling ahhs breathed from a hidden place.

These losses must be.
There is a voice as old as bird, as old as frog song in me
with its own rhythm, season, wisdom.
Earth gave it to people to sing. We call it grief.
And I've been singing it like I was born to.
This evening, again, I've been singing it.

Tome on the Range

She has self published her tenth novel
and I, finally, have a first book of poems.

She arranges a reading at
Tome on the Range,
a bookstore in Las Vegas, New Mexico
where she lives
and I fly west,
rent a car and drive up and east from Albuquerque.

We dress up and go to the bookstore,
talk to the eight or ten people who
come for the reading
about writing when we were children,
and how we keep writing
despite all the reasons to give up.
We read from our books,
sell two or three a piece,
and then go out to dinner
at the nicest place in town.

It is nothing like what we imagined,
but we have done it,
become writers,
and I feel as satisfied as
when I first held the book in my hand
to have shared this humble stage with her
before we run out of time.

Eye surgery, COPD, Crestwood Village North

It is 2012, the Mayan end of the world,
and, after having surgery for a detached retina,
she comes to visit, wanting to tour a few
senior apartment communities.

She tells the women answering our questions
at Benjamin Court and Crestwood Village North
that she doesn't want to live in a place
where she will be urged to leave her room
and participate in yoga and bingo and group sing-alongs.
She just wants a place where she can be left alone to write
and emerge in the evenings occasionally
to play bridge.

She says she has COPD,
the first time I've heard her acknowledge
a diagnosis for the prescribed oxygen tank
which she refuses to use.
She says she doesn't breathe so well
living in the mountains
at an elevation of six thousand feet
and that she isn't huffing and puffing so much
here in Indiana.

When asked when she plans to move,
she says she doesn't want to leave the mountains,
but will move when she can't breathe there anymore.

When asked to tour an apartment
she says, pointing to the floor-plans on the wall,
that she doesn't need to.
"I've moved myself to Iowa
and New Mexico without any help
and without knowing where I would live," she says.
"I don't need to see what color the carpet is,"
using this bravado
to avoid having to walk
from the rental office to the apartment and back
even though we brought her walker with us.

What I Get Up to Write in the Middle of the Night

For someone so angry at aging, she gave herself to it so easily, finding solace by retreating into her body as it shuts down around her, COPD, a walker, while those who might have been her friends are doing yoga and walking on beaches.

For her, fighting her body's aging can be felt only if aging is winning and she is in pain. Then she can curse and swear and feel herself still the hero, the one who defies, against all odds, a foe greater than him. A foe she has bowed down to, in supplication, and assists through her own self-destruction, like the epic warrior, drawing his sword, saying "Bring it on!" to the enemy sent by the gods. The enemy he has waited for all his life. The beloved enemy he needs to overpower him, so that he can die still fighting.

Letting Her Find Her Way

After her visit
she emails to say
another friend has died and
she will move back to Indiana
in the summer of 2014
but she will hate leaving the Southwest's
sagebrush, aspens,
and purple mountains majesty.

I am afraid she won't live that long
and want her to move sooner,
want to read to her as her eyes fail,
old books, her favorites,
which long ago she read to me –
Elsie Piddock Skips in her Sleep,
The Princess and the Goblin
Wild Animals I Have Loved.
I want to sit at her bedside
playing my harp for her
in her final hours.

I want these last connections
for myself and keep them secret.
For she has told me
the wild spot in New Mexico,
the old caldera of a long sleeping volcano,
where she wants her ashes scattered
and so I want for her
what I know she needs –
and has truly chosen –
but also keeps secret –

to stay where she is,
to not suffer the hard grief of moving,
and, like her father, to close her eyes one night
and not wake up,
to feel her spirit breathed – agile and flowing –
from her body
out into the strong, steady pulse
of the mountains,
the dreams of brown bears and ravens,
the deep and infinite stars.

Two Dreams

A few days after Thanksgiving, I dream:

I wake up in my mother's apartment
and know that she is not there.
I no longer have a mother.
The pajamas she was wearing when she died
are folded neatly on the bed.
But everything is happening out of order.
The funeral is already over
and I am just realizing she is gone.
I need to tell our family.
I need to stay longer than planned
sorting her belongings.

Less than two weeks later,
on the dawn of my 50th birthday,
I dream:

A huge cosmic mother's face is slowly
drifting away into star filled space
as Hermione, the smart witch from Harry Potter,
floats on a ski-lift chair
toward a space ship.
Hermione says to the mother-face,
"I will call you back."
The mother-face says,
"I love you."
Hermione: "You are precious. Good bye."
Mother: "Good bye."
And the cosmic mother face begins to fade
but continues to watch
as her daughter turns and boards the ship,
a place of exploration and learning,
on which she will continue her journey.

Emails, Phone Calls and Semicolons

I call her and ask if she will read these poems
and write her own response to them.
I warn her there is anger, hurt, and struggle in these pages.
But there is love here too
and I now know
I need to give these poems to her.
She says she would very much like to read them.

Before Thanksgiving, I email the manuscript.
She can't open docx on her old computer.
She reminds me in phone calls and emails to send a pdf.
Her eyesight is bad; she can't see what she types.
I am looki ng forwrd to reading tjem, she writes.

December begins and I still haven't sent the poems.
My daughter is studying for her
10th grade English final exam.
We call Mom with a question about semicolons;
she explains how they are used
with the clarity of someone who has explained this
to thousands of students.
"Call me any time with semicolon questions!"
she says, pleased to have helped.

She says, to adjust to the idea of moving,
she wants a map of Indianapolis for Christmas.
I buy one at Walmart and mail it to her.

Finally, on Christmas Eve, I email the pdf poems.
We talk on Christmas Day and she says she is reading them.
She asks if I have written any father poems
because living with him
certainly wasn't easy for any of us either.
I say I agree but just haven't yet
found the way to write about him.

On December 29, she emails:
THEre are some stron g poems here.
Somm e things you remmber differently than me.
I wull start writi ng my response;

12:20 am, January 2, 2013

The phone wakes me.
It is my sister.
Rachel, my mother's apartment neighbor,
has just called her to say
she went to check on Mom.
Found her having trouble breathing.
Called the ambulance.
They took her to the hospital.
She is dead.

The Death of Three Animals

When one-eyed, rotting-toothed, drooling, Tom-cat Edward
hid in the corner of the bedroom closet
the day he needed to be put to sleep,
my mother found him and said,
"Animals do this. Go off alone someplace to die."

When Barney the Beagle –
        who always slept snuggled up to me in my bed
        and who I married one afternoon
        with my sister as officiate,
        a teddy-bear ring bearer,
        a dime-store ring,
        and a waltz holding his front paws –
went off as he did every day into the woods
but didn't come home, after two days, then three,
my mother found him
under a tree by the farthest pasture fence
and buried him near the wild strawberries,
telling me when I got home from school,
saying again,
"Animals do that. Go off alone someplace to die."

And when I think of her
sitting alone in her apartment
a thousand, two thousand miles away
from any of her children,
struggling to breathe
and not calling anyone for help,
I see her crouched
in her own dark corner,
beside her own farthest fence,
as the shadows lengthen
and night comes.

Sorting Through My Mother's Belongings

In my mother's apartment,
my brother and sister and I
are sorting through her belongings.

I sort through her writing.
Piles of papers,
manuscript after manuscript,
heaped in with old bills,
donation requests from the Humane Society,
hundreds of unused cat and dog and wild animal note cards,
old journals,
hospital information about her hip replacement,
bank statements.

I sort through recipes
written by hand on yellowed cards
stained with butter and cocoa
and find the now-stiff-with-old-grease
strawberry print apron
she sewed and cooked in
when she was housewife
and mother of small children.

I find a cabinet full of paint, chalk, paper, pencils,
a large box filled with her art:
figure drawings, watercolor landscape sketches,
portraits of cats and cowboys.

I find a box containing letters she saved.
Letters I sent her when I was in college,
letters from her father when she was newly married,
a letter of apology from my father
as they were getting divorced,
dated February 14, 1979,
a few weeks before she moved out.

In a letter I wrote when I was 34,
newly pregnant with Maggie,
but not yet aware I was,
I said to her,
"I now feel more accepting of the patterns,
family history, personal immaturity,
and trial-and-error way of love
that I must bring to my relationships.
My mistakes have been
incentive for maturing me
and I thought you'd like to know
my anger at you has abated
and that I am open
to the next stage of our relationship.
It takes generations to create soul wounds
and generations to heal them
and I am willing to do my part patiently.
Thanks for your help and patience with me over the years."

Lying Awake in Fire

I lie in the dark, unable to sleep,
after two days
of touching and being touched
by the things she made
(in her last week of life,
and when she was a young mother,
and when she first moved here
in her fifties, starting again
the writer's life she dreamed of in college).

I am disturbed by how fast
the last, most creative decades of her life went
and by how my own remaining allotment of time
is suddenly too short
to contain everything I need to do.

And I am awakened and alarmed by
her individual fire,
restless, impatient, pulsing.

I have been holding this fire in my hands all day
with an intimacy not known
since I was a child living in her house
when I grew in it, unconscious of it.

Her spirit, her energy,
prolific, fierce, incandescent,
surrounds me now in the dark night,
alerting, enlivening me,
pushing me toward life,
flaring and burning,
above and below and beside me.

As if some goddess is holding me in the flames,
not to spare me from death,
but to make me forever mortal.

As if I am in her again.
And from her spirit body
I am being further born.

In the First Months After Her Death

I hope for a dream of her
to reassure me she is alright.
But, not sleeping well
I don't remember my dreams.

One night, while lying awake,
I think of the animals she loved
and wonder if,
as she emerged through the tunnel into the light,
her horse Pilot
was among the souls
gathered there to greet her.
And suddenly, I see the image
of her riding bareback
through the pastures of another world,
her body ageless and full of joy,
gleefully galloping away.

One day, a memory comes
of a little pleasure she shared
with me when I visited her last June.
I sat next to her cramped and messy desk
amid piles of paper and coffee cups
and she showed me
her favorite YouTube video
of baby ducks who hatched
on the roof of a bank
(where their imperfect mother had nested)
and a man standing below
gently catching them like feathered baseballs
as they waddled over the threshold,
flightlessly falling.
"I watch this every day," she told me.
"It reminds me of the good in the world."
And this memory comforts me,
reminds me of what was tender in her.

My sleep begins to lengthen.
In dreams I know she is dead but do not see her.

Finally, I dream that,
instead of Charon and his boat over the river Styx,
she is riding in a crowded streetcar in a place like San Francisco.
She is sitting near the open door,
and there are no more seats left.
The streetcar pauses near where I am standing
and she looks right at me,
makes eye contact,
and points her finger at my face emphatically
the way she always did,
fiercely saying, "You tell him…!"
and says more that I don't remember
and then the street car pulls away
and she is talking happily with the others
kicking her feet up in the air
agile and alive in her body
excited about where they are going.

Following

And even when I am in my 70's
and my hip hurts, and my own daughter,
after 4 decades of growing,
is finally choosing her Self
while having to care for and let go of me
(in whatever ways our lives, our personalities allow)
even then, my mother will be in me,
living and changing,
stubbornly undying.

She has always been ahead of me,
on the way to the pear tree, in the mall,
as woman leading child,
as woman entering midlife,
as woman growing old,
onward, onward, marching as to war
through her life, through our lives.

I will let her go, independent and alone,
when this life fades from her
and she climbs the boat with white sails
to voyage beyond where I can see,
beyond where I can imagine.

But she will visit,
in memories, dreams, thoughts,
planted in my body, like seeds that will
wake only when I come to
the twists in life's road she traveled before me,
only as I reach the age she was
when she came to these choices, these crossroads.

And I will go deep down into her story bravely singing,
I will wrestle with what was monster and what was milk in her.
Fears will surface as I walk
from the middle of the world toward my future.

And sometimes there will come from her,
a gift, a taste of something golden, ripe, living, unexpected,
and I will follow her,
follow her,
follow her,
this woman who has been galloping, marching,
loosing and finding her way,
hurrying impatiently, limping with her cane,
pushing angrily against her walker
toward this place where we begin,
this tree of life,
this Great Mother,
this living universe
of fruitful darkness
and delicious light,
here at birth, in life,
and on the other side of death.

Author Biography

Poet Liza Hyatt is the author of *Under My Skin,* (WordTech Editions, 2012), *Seasons of the Star Planted Garden* (Stonework Press, 1999), and *Stories Made of World* (Finishing Line Press, 2013). She has been published in various regional, national, and international journals and anthologies including Tipton Poetry Journal, Painted Bride Quarterly, THEMA, Black River Review, Pudding Magazine, Indiannual 4, 5, and 6, Flying Island, Branches Magazine, and England's Tears in the Fence. In 2006, Hyatt received an Individual Artist Project Grant from the Indiana Arts Commission.

Liza is an art therapist (ATR-BC, LMHC) and adjunct professor at both St. Mary of the Woods College and Herron School of Art and Design. She hosts a monthly poetry reading at the Lawrence Art Center on the east side of Indianapolis. She is the author of *Art of the Earth: Ancient Art for a Green Future* (Authorhouse, 2007) an art-based eco-psychology workbook. For more information, visit www.lizahyatt.wordpress.com.

Liza's mother, Jane Hyatt self-published over a dozen books, including novels, short story collections, and a memoir of her years as an English teacher. Her final three books – *More Baba, A Horse Named Sulie,* and *The Adventures of Hap Farr and Henry Hawk* – were completed posthumously with Liza's help. Jane's books are available through Authorhouse and Xlibirs.

Also by Chatter House Press

beyond first words
Penny Dunning

Street Girls Have Guns
Gregg DeBoor

Battle Scarred
Jason Ammermon

Almost Music From Between Places
Steven R. Roberts

Some Poems To Be Read Out Loud
Richard Pflum

Muntu Kuntu Energy
Mwatabu Okantah

World of Mortal Light
Virginia Slachman

Hot Type Cold Read
Tony Brewer

Written in the Dish Pit
Adam Henze

Inside Virgil's Garage
Lindsey Martin-Bowen

Made in the USA
Charleston, SC
11 July 2014